"Change your internal story and you
will change your life"

TONY ROBBINS

"I am beautiful & timeless at every
age. I am enough"

JENNIFER LOPEZ

"Music is my life, the fame is
inside of me"

LADY GAGA

Lucky Girl Syndrome is the latest Manifestation trend that's supporting people all over the world to Manifest their Dreams into Reality through affirming and believing that they are Lucky.

Could you do with a dose of Luck?

This Affirmation Oracle Book has 200 Affirmations to support you with receiving more Luck, more Magic and more Miracles into your life.

These 200 Affirmations have been created to support you with:

- Manifesting your Dream Life
- Manifesting Love
- Manifesting Money
- Manifesting a GLOW UP

These Affirmations have been specifically created to align you to the frequency of LUCK and to align you with the vibration of your desires.

BELIEVE you are worth it and you will get it.

"I am a Magnet for Miracles"

How to use this Oracle Book::

Each Affirmation has a page number 1 – 200

1. First thing in the Morning & Last thing at Night pick the first number that comes into your head between 1 and 200

2.. Ask your Subconscious to clear any resistance and to accept this Affirmation as your new truth. Turn to the page and read the Affirmation allowed 3 times (If you can, do it in front of a mirror)

3. Ensure you are in a good mood and if you aren't get yourself into one

4. Then close your eyes and repeat the affirmation for as long as you desire but no less than 60 seconds

5. Visualise yourself embodying the Affirmation, feel every word you are saying (The Affirmation is the rocket, the feeling is the fuel, so it's important to really feel and believe that this is your Truth)

6. Believe it or you won't receive it, you HAVE to BELIEVE you are worthy of all the things the Universe wants you to have

7. Trust YOU ARE WORTHY, everybody deserves good fortune

8. To take it a level further you can repeatedly write the affirmation in a journal and even be more specific with scripting

9. If doubt creeps in throughout the day or your vibe starts to drop reaffirm the affirmation

10. Enhance the magic even further and use our FREE Activation Meditation (details available at the back of the book)

You are the Creator of your own Reality, the more you BELIEVE you are worthy of Luck the more Luck you will receive.

Always remember the more grateful you are, the more you will have to be grateful for.

Sometimes you just need to remember how Lucky you already are.

"Universe show me how

Lucky I am?"

EVERYTHING IS ALWAYS WORKING OUT FOR ME BECAUSE I HAVE THE POWER TO MANIFEST ANYTHING!

TODAY, NO PERSON, PLACE OR THING CAN IRRITATE OR ANNOY ME!

I RECOGNISE THAT I AM THE CREATOR OF MY OWN REALITY AND I WILL USE MY POWER TO MANIFEST WHAT I WANT!

THE MORE LOVE I GIVE THE MORE I RECEIVE!

MY POSITIVE MINDSET & ATTITUDE IS OPENING NEW DOORS FOR ME!

I ALLOW MYSELF TO HAVE THE GOOD THINGS IN LIFE AND I ENJOY THEM!

I AM HERE FOR A DIVINE PURPOSE

I RELEASE STRUGGLE

I AM HERE TO BE FREE!

EVERYTHING THAT I DESIRE IS MAKING ITS WAY TO ME!

I NO LONGER LIVE TO SURVIVE

I LIVE TO THRIVE!

I AM BEAUTIFUL AND FEEL RECOGNISED FOR MY BEAUTY THAT RADIATES FROM WITHIN!

MY EMOTIONS ARE MY RESPONSIBILITY AND I MAKE SURE I CHOOSE TO BE HAPPY REGARDLESS OF MY CIRCUMSTANCES!

I WILL GLOW UP NO MATTER WHAT!

I RELEASE ALL WORRIES ABOUT MY IMPERFECTIONS

I AM BEAUTIFUL AND PERFECTLY IMPERFECT!

I EMBRACE MY FLAWS BECAUSE NOBODY IS PERFECT!

I KNOW THAT TRUE BEAUTY COMES FROM WITHIN AND I RADIATE BEAUTY FROM THE INSIDE OUT!

I AM A MAGNET FOR LOVE AND POSITIVE ATTENTION!

THE MORE I LOVE MYSELF THE MORE BEAUTIFUL I BECOME!

I'M WORTHY ENOUGH TO FOLLOW MY DREAMS AND MANIFEST MY DESIRES!

MY SOUL IS READY TO LIVE THE LIFE OF MY DREAMS!

19

MONEY COMES TO ME IN EXPECTED AND UNEXPECTED WAYS!

I AM WORTHY OF FINANCIAL SUCCESS

MY SUCCESS IS INEVITABLE!

I AM ATTRACTING LOVE INTO MY LIFE

IT IS SAFE FOR ME TO LET IT IN!

IF I CAN FEEL IT, VISUALISE IT & BELIEVE IT, I CAN MANIFEST IT!

I THINK POSITIVE THOUGHTS & MANIFEST POSITIVE THINGS INTO MY LIFE!

I TRUST THAT THE WHOLE UNIVERSE IS CONSPIRING IN MY FAVOR!

THINGS ARE ALWAYS WORKING OUT IN MY BEST INTEREST!

EVERYDAY I AM BECOMING A BETTER VERSION OF MYSELF!

I AM CAPABLE OF OVER-COMING OBSTACLES THAT STAND IN MY WAY!

IT IS WITHIN MY POWER TO CREATE A SUCCESSFUL FUTURE!

I HAVE THE DISCIPLINE TO MAKE THE RIGHT CHOICES NOW TO ENJOY AN EASIER FUTURE!

LIFE GETS TO BE EASY BECAUSE I CHOOSE TO LIVE AN EASY, BREEZY, BEAUTIFUL LIFE!

I CHOOSE TO FOCUS ON WHAT I DESIRE NO MATTER WHAT MY CURRENT REALITY LOOKS LIKE!

I AM THE MASTER OF MY WEALTH

MONEY HAS EARS AND HEARS WHEN I CALL IT!

I AM GRATEFUL THAT THE MONEY I SPEND COMES BACK TO ME TEN-FOLD!

I CONSTANTLY ATTRACT ATTRACT OPPORTUNITIES THAT I ACT ON AND CREATE WEALTH FROM!

I AM WORTHY OF HEALING MY TRAUMA

I AM WORTHY OF RELEASING MY KARMA!

MONEY COMES TO ME EASILY

MONEY COMES TO ME FREELY

MONEY COMES TO ME ABUNDANTLY!

THE MORE MONEY I MAKE THE MORE GOOD I CAN DO!

I TRUST THAT I NEVER MISS A TRICK!

THE WARRIOR WITHIN ME HAS ALREADY WON!

I AM FREE FROM MY MISTAKES AND HAVE LEARNT THE LESSONS I NEEDED TO LEARN!

ALL LACK, LIMITATION AND FAILURE ARE WIPED FROM MY MIND!

I DESERVE TO SHINE MY LIGHT BRIGHT

IT IS SAFE FOR ME TO BE SEEN!

I AM FOREVER YOUNG & BECOMING MORE BEAUTIFUL EACH DAY!

MY BODY IS BEAUTIFUL NO MATTER WHAT SIZE I AM!

MY WEIGHT MAY FLUCTUATE BUT MY WORTH DOES NOT!

MY SKIN IS GLOWING AND RADIATES BEAUTY!

I LIVE A LIFE FILLED WITH BEAUTY & GRACE!

I AM HEALTHY, HAPPY AND FULL OF POSITIVE ENERGY!

I AM ADMIRED BY THOSE AROUND ME

PEOPLE ARE ALWAYS INTERESTED IN HEARING WHAT I HAVE TO SAY!

I
HAVE
EVERYTHING
I NEED TO
SUCCEED
IN LIFE!

TODAY I CHOOSE TO PLAY BIG BECAUSE THE UNIVERSE FAVOURS THE BRAVE!

I CANNOT FAIL AT BEING MYSELF!

MY PAST DOES NOT DEFINE ME

FROM NOW ON I FOCUS ON THE PRESENT AND THE FUTURE!

I RELEASE FEELINGS OF WORRY AND CONCERN AND TRUST IN THE PROCESS!

I WELCOME MORE HAPPINESS & JOY INTO MY LIFE ON A DAILY BASIS!

I FULLY ACCEPT ALL OF MYSELF AND KNOW THAT I WILL NEVER BE TOO MUCH FOR THE RIGHT PERSON!

I RADIATE POSITIVE ENERGY AND DETTACH MYSELF FROM ANY NEGATIVITY!

I AM
ALIGNING WITH
MY HIGHER SELF

I AM
ALIGNING WITH
MY GOALS

I AM
MANIFESTING
MAGIC!

I KNOW MYSELF BETTER THAN ANYONE ELSE KNOWS ME!

WHAT I THINK ABOUT MYSELF IS THE ONLY OPINION THAT MATTERS!

MONEY LOVES ME

MONEY WAS DESIGNED TO SUPPORT ME

IT IS NOT JUDGING ME

IT IS RESPONDING TO ME

I TRUST THAT
IF THINGS
AREN'T
WORKING OUT
FOR ME AS I
EXPECTED IT'S
BECAUSE
SOMETHING
BETTER IS
COMING!

I ONLY FOCUS ON WHAT I WANT AND NOT ON WHAT I DON'T WANT!

I AM STEPPING INTO THE HIGHEST VERSION OF MYSELF!

I TRUST THAT IT WILL WORK OUT BETTER THAN I COULD HAVE EVER IMAGINED!

THE UNIVERSE IS RIGGED IN MY FAVOUR!

67

MY
REALITY IS
STARTING
TO BECOME
A
DREAM
COME
TRUE!

HOW AM I ALWAYS SO LUCKY?

WEALTH IS MY BIRTHRIGHT & ABUNDANCE IS MY DESTINY!

THE LOVE I SEEK IS SEEKING ME!

THE UNIVERSE ALWAYS PROVIDES ME WITH EVERYTHING I NEED!

I AM CONFIDENT IN MYSELF AND WHAT I BRING TO THE TABLE!

I NO LONGER
HAVE TO PROVE
ANYTHING TO
ANYONE
BECAUSE THOSE
THAT MIND
DON'T MATTER
AND THOSE
THAT MATTER
DON'T MIND!

I LOVINGLY AND PEACEFULLY CALL ALL OF MY POWER BACK TO ME NOW!

ANY NEGATIVE ENERGY SENT MY WAY I SEND BACK TO THE SENDER WITH LOVE!

TODAY IS GOING TO BE THE BEST DAY OF MY LIFE!

MONEY COMES TO ME EASILY

MONEY COMES TO ME FAST

MONEY LOVES MY COMPANY

WHEN MONEY COMES IT LASTS!

I AM COMMITTED TO SHOWING UP FOR MYSELF AND FORGIVE MYSELF FOR ALL OF THE TIMES I DIDN'T!

I EMBRACE WHAT MAKES ME UNIQUE

I LOVE WHO I AM

I LOVE WHO I AM BECOMING!

I AM ABOUT TO EXPERIENCE WIN AFTER WIN AFTER WIN

MY TIME IS NOW I JUST HAVE TO BELIEVE IT!

I LOVE AND ACCEPT MY MIND AND BODY

I WILL NOURISH AND CHERISH THEM WITH LOVING THOUGHTS TODAY AND ALWAYS!

IT IS SAFE FOR ME TO RECEIVE THE THINGS I DESIRE

I BELIEVE IN MY ABILITY TO ACHIEVE THEM!

I AM MAGIC ON LEGS

MY WORD IS MY WAND!

THERE HAS BEEN AND WILL ONLY EVER BE ONE ME!

I NO LONGER LONGER LET MY THOUGHTS CONTROL ME BECAUSE I CONTROL MY THOUGHTS!

I TRUST THAT THE UNIVERSE HAS MY BACK TODAY AND EVERY OTHER DAY!

I AM ONE OF A KIND AND WORTHY OF A LOVE THAT IS DIVINE!

UNIVERSE, SHOW ME HOW GOOD TODAY CAN BE!

MY ENERGY IS MAGNETIC

I ATTRACT THE RIGHT PEOPLE INTO MY LIFE AND REPEL THE WRONG PEOPLE!

GREAT THINGS ARE ALWAYS HAPPENING TO ME UNEXPECTEDLY!

I AM DIVINELY GUIDED AND PROTECTED AT ALL TIMES!

I AM SO HAPPY AND GRATEFUL THAT MONEY COMES TO ME IN INCREASING QUANTITIES THROUGH MULTIPLE SOURCES ON A CONTINUOUS BASIS!

I AM SO PROUD OF HOW FAR I HAVE COME AND I AM EXCITED THAT THE BEST IS YET TO COME!

I AM ABOUT TO BECOME THE HAPPIEST, HEALTHIEST, WEALTHIEST AND MOST HEALED VERSION OF MYSELF!

I AM
IRRESISTIBLE

I AM
MAGNETIC

I ATTRACT
LOVE EASILY!

I
BREATHE
IN LOVE
AND
BREATHE
OUT
FEAR!

THE PARTNER I SEEK IS ALSO SEEKING ME

I NOW RELEASE ANY BLOCKS THAT ARE STANDING INBETWEEN US!

I AM BECOMING THE BEST VERSION OF MYSELF AS THERE ARE NO OBSTACLES I CANNOT OVERCOME!

I AM GOING TO FIGURE EVERYTHING OUT AND IT'S GOING TO BE SO WORTH IT WHEN I DO!

I DESERVE TO BE LOVED EVEN IF I AM STILL LEARNING TO LOVE MYSELF!

I AM SO MUCH MORE THAN WHAT I HAVE BEEN TOLD I AM!

I DON'T NEED TO BE LIKE THEM I JUST NEED TO BE LIKED ME!

THERE
IS NO
COMPETITION
BECAUSE
NOBODY
DOES IT
LIKE ME!

I RELEASE ANYTHING & ANYONE THAT DOES NOT ALIGN WITH MY VISION AND MY FUTURE!

I LOVE THE WAY MY BODY LOOKS

I LOVE HOW MY BODY FEELS

I LOVE THAT MY BODY IS MINE!

I'M SO POWERFUL

I'M SO CONFIDENT

I'M UNSTOPPABLE EVERY SINGLE DAY!

I WELCOME FINANCIAL, MENTAL, EMOTIONAL, SPIRITUAL & PHYSICAL STABILITY INTO MY LIFE!

MY CHAKRAS ARE ALIGNED

MY BODY IS DEFINED

THE UNIVERSE IS ON MY SIDE

I AM PERFECTLY DESIGNED!

I AM COMMITTED TO MY VISION BECAUSE THAT'S THE LIFE I CHOSE FOR MYSELF!

IF IT CAN HAPPEN FOR THEM IT CAN HAPPEN FOR ME!

I AM AN POWERFUL MAGNET FOR MIRACLES!

I RADIATE CONFIDENCE

I GLOW WITH BEAUTY

I MOVE WITH GRACE!

I
RELEASE
ALL
NEGATIVITY
AND
WELCOME
ONLY
POSITIVITY!

MY MIND IS A MAGNET

WHAT I THINK I ATTRACT

I CHOOSE TO THINK ONLY THINGS I WISH TO ATTRACT!

I AM IN
CHARGE
OF MY
HAPPINESS

I WILL
NOT LET
ANYTHING
OUTSIDE
OF MYSELF
CONTROL ME!

MONEY IS A NEUTRAL RESOURCE

IT HAS NO FREE WILL

I GOES AND FLOWS WHERE I TELL IT TO!

I CREATE AND MAINTAIN BOUNDARIES THAT PROTECT ME AND SUPPORT ME!

I ACCEPT MYSELF FOR WHO I AM

I LET GO OF ANY JUDGMENT & CRITICISM THAT RESIDES WITHIN ME!

MY LIFE
IS 100% MY
RESPONSIBILITY

THE BETTER
I BECOME
THE BETTER MY
LIFE BECOMES!

I
CHOOSE
TO
STRIVE
FOR
PROGRESS
OVER
PERFECTION!

I BREATHE
IN
POSITIVITY
&
BREATHE
OUT
NEGATIVITY!

I AM DEDICATED TO MY GROWTH

I AM COMMITTED TO LEARNING TO LOVE WHO I AM MORE AND MORE EVERYDAY!

I FOCUS ON WHAT I CAN CONTROL AND I LET GO OF WHAT I CAN'T!

I
BREATHE
IN
COURAGE
AND
EXHALE
DOUBT!

MY
LOVE
FOR
MYSELF
IS
BOLD
FIERCE
AND
UNCONDITIONAL!

I
CHOOSE
FAITH
OVER FEAR

LOVE OVER
HATE

PEACE OVER
PERFECTION!

IT IS SAFE FOR ME TO SPEAK MY TRUTH

WHAT I HAVE TO SAY MATTERS!

I HAVE THE MAGICAL ABILITY TO ATTRACT LARGE SUMS OF MONEY THAT I GET TO KEEP!

I AM IN ALIGNMENT WITH MY TRUE HEARTS DESIRES!

I FOCUS ON THE THOUGHTS THAT MAKE ME FEEL GOOD AND LET GO OF THE ONES THAT DON'T!

I KNOW I'M GOOD AT WHAT I DO

I KNOW THAT I ALWAYS FIGURE THINGS OUT!

I AM GRATEFUL FOR MY HEALTHY BODY AND CONTINUE TO CHOOSE TO MAKE HEALTHY CHOICES!

IT IS EASY FOR ME TO MAINTAIN A BODY THAT I ADORE!

I LOVE MY UNIQUE STYLE

WHAT I WEAR REPRESENTS HOW I WANT TO EXPRESS MYSELF!

I LOVE MY HAIR

IT IS THE DREAM HAIR I HAVE ALWAYS WANTED!

I AM A MAGNET FOR LOVE AND POSITIVE ATTENTION!

I AM SO PROTECTED THAT I TRUST THAT WHATEVER LEAVES COMES BACK EVEN BETTER!

I CALL BACK MY POWER WITH LOVE & GRACE FROM EVERY PERSON, PLACE OR THING FROM ALL LIFETIMES & DIMENSIONS ACROSS ALL TIME AND SPACE!

REGARDLESS OF MY PAST I AM WORTHY OF LOVE AND ALLOW LOVE TO COME INTO MY LIFE IN A MAGICAL WAY!

I AM WORTHY OF A DEEP AND FULFILLING LOVE, TODAY AND ALWAYS!

I LOVE THE PERSON I AM BECOMING

I AM A UNIQUE EXPRESSION OF THE DIVINE AND CANNOT BE REPLACED!

I ALLOW NEW LEVELS OF LOVE TO ENTER MY LIFE, MY MIND AND MY HEART!

I GIVE MYSELF PERMISSION TO SHOW UP BIG TODAY AND MAKE THINGS HAPPEN!

I FORGIVE MYSELF FOR BEING SO HARD ON MYSELF

I FORGIVE MYSELF FOR NOT DOING THE THINGS I SAID I WOULD

I RELEASE THIS PRESSURE I HAVE PUT ON MYSELF!

I AM A MASTER AT MANIFESTING

I AM THE LUCKIEST PERSON I KNOW!

I
ALLOW
MYSELF TO
RECEIVE
WONDERFUL
THINGS!

IT'S ALL SO EASY AND IT'S ALREADY DONE

I CHOOSE TO RELAX, CHILL OUT AND LET IT ALL COME!

THERE IS NOTHING I NEED TO GO BACK AND LIVE OVER, OR FIX, OR FEEL REGRET ABOUT BECAUSE EVERY PART OF MY LIFE UNFOLDED JUST RIGHT!

I AM A VIBRATIONAL MATCH TO THAT WHICH I DESIRE!

I CHOOSE TO FREE MYSELF FROM MY NEGATIVE THOUGHTS SO I CAN LIVE A LIFE OF FREEDOM!

I AM HAPPY WITH WHERE I AM YET EAGER FOR MORE

I HAVE ONE FOOT IN GRATITUDE & ONE FOOT IN DESIRE!

INSTEAD OF OVER-THINKING, RUSHING & STRESSING I ALIGN MY FAITH WITH DIVINE TIMING!

INSTANT MANIFESTATIONS BECOME A DAILY OCCURRENCE NOW I'M NOT CONTRADICTING MY OWN VIBRATIONAL DESIRES!

I CHOOSE TO FOCUS ON THE GOOD BECAUSE WHEN I FOCUS ON THE GOOD THE GOOD GETS BETTER!

I SURVIVED BECAUSE THE FIRE INSIDE OF ME BURNED BRIGHTER THAN THE FIRE AROUND ME!

I PUSH MYSELF DAILY SO THAT MY FUTURE SELF WILL THANK ME!

I AM DESERVING OF A LIFE FILLED WITH LUXURY!

IT IS MY DOMINANT INTENT TO FEEL GOOD NO MATTER WHAT HAPPENS TODAY!

I CHOOSE
TO SHINE
WHETHER
THEY LIKE ME
OR NOT

WHAT THEY
THINK OF ME
NO LONGER
MATTERS
TO ME!

I AM ONE OF THE HAPPIEST PEOPLE ON THE PLANET!

I HAVE A LOVING & SUPPORTIVE FAMILY THAT ADORE ME!

I HAVE FOUND MY SOUL FRIENDS WHO SUPPORT ME, ADORE ME AND LOVE ME!

I AM COMMITTED TO INNER PEACE, GROWTH, SELF LOVE AND GRATITUDE!

ANYTHING IS POSSIBLE FOR ME IF I BELIEVE IN MYSELF!

I CHOOSE TO LIVE AN EASY LIFE

A LIFE FILLED WITH LOVE & FREEDOM!

I AM EXPERIENCING EXACTLY WHAT IS NEEDED FOR MY HEALING, GROWTH & AWAKENING!

I AM THE CREATOR OF MY MOOD THEREFORE I AM THE CREATOR OF MY DAY!

I HEAR MY INTUITION CLEARLY AND ALLOW IT TO GUIDE ME WITH GRACE!

I AM WHOLE

I AM STRONG

I AM HAPPY

I AM BLESSED

I AM SEEN

I AM HEARD

I AM KNOWN!

I AM GRATEFUL
FOR MY HEALTH
MY BODY
TO SEE
TO HEAR
TO SPEAK
TO LIVE
TO BREATHE!

I AM GRATEFUL FOR ALL THAT I HAVE NO MATTER HOW BIG OR SMALL BECAUSE THERE ARE MANY THAT AREN'T SO BLESSED!

I BELIEVE
IN THE POWER
OF GRATITUDE

I AM
GRATEFUL
FOR ALL THAT
I HAVE AND
ALL THAT IS
COMING!

I AM GRATEFUL FOR BEING ABLE TO CREATE A LIFE THAT I LOVE!

I AM COMING CLOSER INTO ALIGNMENT WITH WHAT I WANT!

I LOVE KNOWING THAT I AM THE CREATOR OF MY REALITY AND THAT IT IS OK FOR ME TO DREAM BIG!

I DESERVE TO BE LOVED A LITTLE DEEPER AND APPRECIATED A LITTLE MORE!

IT FEELS GOOD FOR ME TO KNOW THAT I CAN BE, DO AND HAVE ANYTHING I CHOOSE!

I AM SO LUCKY

GREAT THINGS ALWAYS HAPPEN TO ME UNEXPECTEDLY

I AM SURROUNDED BY BLESSINGS!

I HAVE STOPPED LOOKING FOR REASONS TO FEEL BAD AND CHOOSE TO FOCUS ON THINGS THAT MAKE ME FEEL GOOD!

I HAVE STOPPED SEARCHING FOR MY FAULTS AND ONLY FOCUS ON THE GIFTS & STRENGTHS THAT I HAVE!

I HAVE FOUND ULTIMATE FREEDOM LIVING A LIFE I LOVE EVERYDAY!

MY LIFE IS AS GOOD AS MY MINDSET

I CHOOSE TO ONLY FOCUS ON WHAT MAKES ME FEEL GOOD!

I NO LONGER FEEL THE NEED TO PUT PEOPLE ABOVE ME!

I AM WORTHY OF A DEEP AND FULFILLING LOVE TODAY AND ALWAYS!

MONEY IS A TOOL THAT I CAN USE TO MAKE MY LIFE BETTER

MONEY WORKS FOR ME!

ALL OF MY DEBTS AND BILLS ARE PAID UNDER GRACE IN PERFECT WAYS!

I AM MEANT TO BE SUCCESSFUL

I AM MEANT TO SHARE THE THINGS INSIDE OF ME WITH THE WORLD!

I AM GOING TO SHOW UP AND GIVE IT MY BEST EVEN WHEN I DON'T FEEL LIKE IT!

THERE IS AN ENDLESS SUPPLY OF MONEY

I HAVE MORE MONEY THAN I KNOW WHAT TO DO WITH!

I AM ENOUGH JUST AS I AM AND WILL NOT ALLOW OTHERS TO MAKE ME FEEL ANY DIFFERENTLY!

I WILL NOT SETTLE BECAUSE I KNOW I WAS BORN FOR THIS!

I CHOOSE TO BE THE BEST

BEST

HAVE THE BEST

RECEIVE THE BEST!

I RECOGNISE WHEN I AM IN A LOW VIBRATION AND CHOOSE TO SHIFT INTO A HIGHER VIBRATION EASILY AND EFFORTLESSLY!

I LOOK AT OTHERS SUCCESSES AND KNOW THAT IF THEY CAN DO IT THEN I CAN DO IT!

I AM SO LUCKY TO LIVE THIS LIFE

LIFE IS PRECIOUS AND I CHOOSE TO LOVE LIVING EVERY DAY!

WHEN I FEEL GOOD I ALLOW MYSELF TO STAY IN THAT FEELING FOR AS LONG AS POSSIBLE!

IT IS IMPORTANT FOR ME TO TAKE CARE OF MYSELF BEFORE I TAKE CARE OF OTHERS!

GREAT THINGS ARE BEING MANIFESTED INTO MY LIFE

I AM GRATEFUL THAT I HAVE ALL THAT I HAVE WANTED

EVERY DAY IN EVERY WAY MY LIFE GETS BETTER & BETTER!

About the Author:

Sammy Shiers is a
Mindset, Mindfulness & Spiritual Coach
who believes that if you master
your Mindset & Believe in yourself,
you can create Magic and achieve Miracles.

She is the founder of The Frequency Academy where
she helps people all over the world become the best
version of themselves through mastering their
Mindset, Healing, Self Love,
Self Awareness & Self Acceptance.

Each purchase gets you **FREE** access to our Lucky
Tapping Activation & Meditation to support you with
Manifesting more **LUCK** into your life.

Head over to

www.thefrequencyacademy.co.uk/mindset

Printed in Great Britain
by Amazon

17813006R00119